WRITTEN BY
MURRAY McCAIN

DESIGNED AND ILLUSTRATED BY
JOHN ALCORN

AMMO

Books! by Murray McCain and John Alcorn

First published 1962

All original content is © Topipittori, Milano 2012. All Rights Reserved.
Topipittori, viale Isonzo 16, 20135 Milano, Italia. www.topipittori.it

ISBN: 9781623260200
Library of Congress Control Number:
2013935433

Printed in China

For more information on AMMO Books, please visit
www.ammobooks.com

For Toye and Murray and Candida

WITH LOVE

What is a book

A book is many, many things,
at least ten thousand.

A BOOK IS
for colouring

for looking at

For Writing In

and most important
**FOR
READING**

But **WHAT** is a book?

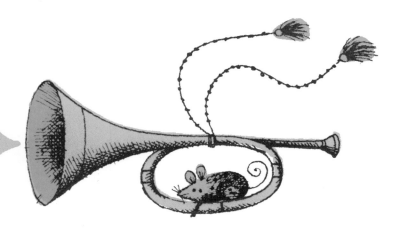

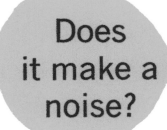
Does it make a noise?

What does it look like and
what does it do?

Can it  to you?

What does it feel like and
what does it say?
If you bark at it, will it run?

Why is it a book and where
did it come from?
Will it be there next week?
Will it go?

First of All

(Turn page)

Books are both outside

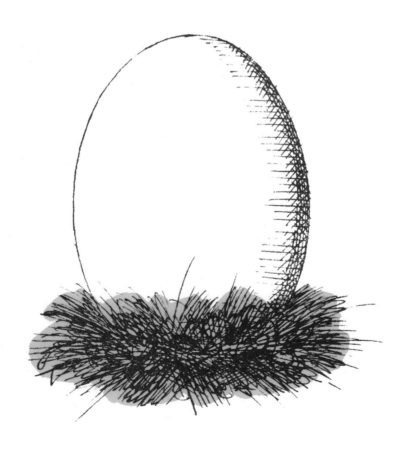

&
Inside

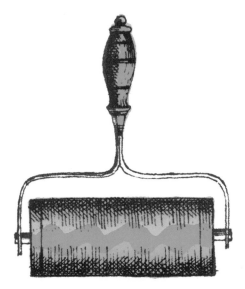

Outside a book is:
binding, thread, glue, paper and ink.
Usually they smell very good.

**They can be any colour, except
the glue and thread**
(Can you find them? Are they invisible?)
and the ink, which is mostly black.

OUTSIDE

the outside of a book
is sometimes a dust jacket
to keep it clean.

At times it can
also tell you in a clear
way just exactly
what is inside.

There is a reason for nearly everything.

Most books are just right for holding.

(Some are too heavy but none are too light.)
They can come in
all shapes and sizes.

Each piece of paper
in a book is two pages.
Like this.

There is a page on each side.
They are both necessary.

What is
not
finished on
one is

 continued on the next.

Thousands of new books are published every year. Printing presses roll night and day to keep them coming. Trains go eighty miles an hour to deliver them everywhere. The bookseller opens big boxes of books and puts them on his shelf and says: "Here they are!" The postman wears out his shoes bringing them up to front doors. And while one book is being opened up, another is being written.

A long time ago, books were put together by monks who copied each one by hand. That was a good way to do things too.

BOOKS!
BOOKS!
BOOKS!

What else is a book?

AH!

There are all kinds of books

INSIDE

And that is where they are
even prettier.

THERE ARE
BOOKS ABOUT

wizards
the silver nutmeg
Scrooge
merry-go-rounds
battleships
the Amazon
mermaids
Pooh
Ethelred the Unready
the Secret Garden
Big Claus and Little Claus
Rome
Mozart
the wind in the willows
space ships
puppies
Arabian nights
the Cat that Walked by Himself
the Caspian Sea
the Tailor of Gloucester
emeralds
the little red engine
Rose Red
Billy Bunter

Oz
Black Beauty
the girl from nowhere
El Greco
ghosts
dragons
Borrowers
St. Nicholas
the emperor's new clothes
boys
snarks
Swallows & Amazons
Paddington
Johnny Crow's Garden
giants
Eloise
Doctor Dolittle
sailors
Peter and the wolf
Lilliputians

the little prince
the Pyrenees
San Francisco
butterflies
Old King Cole
the red balloon
lions
and good King Wenceslas

& OTHER THINGS

Peter Pan is in a book.
Have you learned to fly?

& Books
To
COLOUR

and
Books
to help
you sing and
play the
celesta and the
concertina
and the guitar . . .

...and picture books that
may show another
boy or girl in Peru or
Port Said or Siam,
LOOKING AT YOU

Books are books
INSIDE
because they have words,
and sometimes music,
and sometimes pictures.

Did you ever see a book
without a word?
Words are to help you
understand books.

There are all kinds of words

HARD
WORDS

planetarium
ache
wrong
Adeste Fideles
geography
if
mumps
almost
twenty-eight plus nine hundred
and seventy-three
practise
Rumpelstiltskin
must
hippopotamus
wait
extraordinary
misunderstand
myrrh
anemone
Confucius
long distance
Paderewski
truly
antidisestablishmentarianism

dance

April

kites

Bambi

Oh, Susannah

birthday

Sheep May Safely Graze

Once upon a time

gingerbread house

Christmas tree

brass band

yes

parade

baked Alaska

daffodils

play ball

good morning

show boat

Greensleeves

poem

snowman

kiss

rainbow

grandfather clock

Japanese lantern

grow

rosemary

the beach

pennies

lollipops

FUNNY WORDS

clown

Pogo

zoo

camomile

firecrackers

Yogi Bear

Falstaff

Boston Charlie

weeping willow

porpoise

toadstool

Kalamazoo

Ulysses

pineapple upside-down cake

gnus

cuckoo

blellum

purple cow

Sellenger's Round

Dr. Seuss

Huckleberry Finn

abracadabra

Beelzebub

Sad words like

& WORDS TO THINK ABOUT

subtract

mystery

shouldn't

perfect

imagine

manhood

Greece

myth

choose

gentle

idea

Shakespeare

Capricorn

Mother

give

can't

the Prime Minister

everyone

please

what to do now

puzzle

why

magic

Alice in Wonderland

right

what to do when you grow up

Your name is a word.
And mine.
Every word has a meaning,
unless it is
Jabberwocky

Your name means

YOU

WORDS WORDS WORDS WORDS

Put
them
all
together
and you
are
reading.

Words are words because
they have letters.
Did you ever see a word
without a letter?
Letters are to help you
understand words.

There are all kinds of letters. Big letters and little letters, rounded letters and squared letters, straight letters and crooked letters, and letters that are combinations.

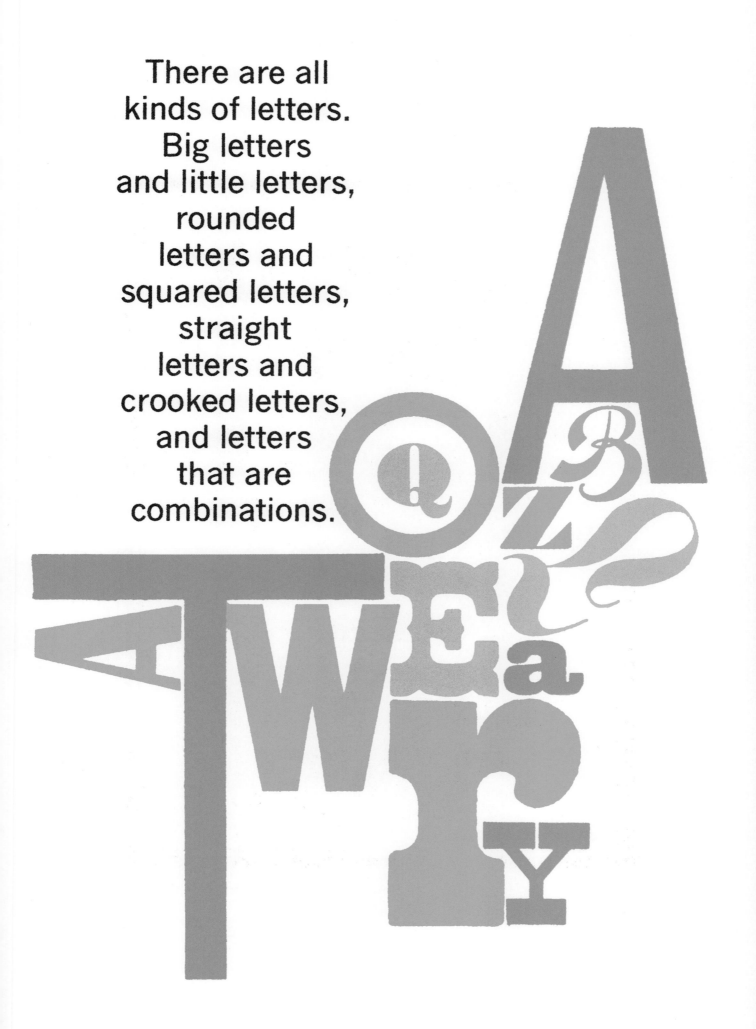

Twenty-six in all.

Put them all together and
you are writing.

Sometimes you need help.
That is what
full stops

• • •

commas

,,,

question marks

and exclamation marks

are for.
Full stops and commas give
the words a rest.
A question mark waits
for an answer.
And an exclamation mark is
to give you a surprise!

Words, letters, full stops,
commas, question marks and
exclamation marks.
Put them all together and
they make books!
Books are written by people like

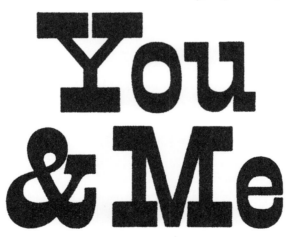

You
& Me

A book is full of surprises,
feelings and learning
and what growing up is like
and loving and all the
really big things there are.

All we know of lots of long-ago people
—who they were and what they
were like and what they did and how
they lived—is in a book.
Some books are about things that
happened a hundred years ago.
And some books are about things
that may happen day after tomorrow.
Anyway, a book will tell you if
you want to find out.
The whole world is in books.

A goat thinks books are made to eat.
But it is a known fact that
goats don't know how to read.

aren't allowed in libraries.
DO YOU KNOW WHY

Libraries are
full of

old
books
and new
books
red
books
and blue
books
sad
books
and gay
books
work
books
and play
books—
waiting for
you to
read them.

A book is like a friend,
because when you read
you feel close to someone.
Some books are like
valentines.

They seem to say

I LOVE YOU

If a book is yours,
you can put your name in it.

A book is like another room,
or another town, or
another world, where someone is
waiting to speak to you.

You can love a person in a book,
or a cat in a book,
or a house in a book.
You can even love a book.
INSIDE AND OUT

What is a book?